Puppy Love - World's Cutest Puppies

Speedy Publishing LLC
40 E. Main St. #1156
Newark, DE 19711

www.speedypublishing.com

Copyright 2014
9781681271934
First Printed December 3, 2014

Puppy Facts...

Each year, there are 6.2 million puppies born in the United States

Puppy Facts...

The most popular dog breed in the U.S. in 2013 was the Labrador retriever.

Puppy Facts...

Puppies are born without teeth.

Puppy Facts...

The second most popular breed in 2013 was the German shepherd.

Puppy Facts...

Puppies are born unable to hear or smell. They are unable to smell until about three weeks after birth.

Puppy Facts...

Newborn puppies spend about 90 percent of their first week sleeping. Puppies follow a sleep schedule similar to that of a newborn human. The average human newborn sleeps 16 hours in a 24-hour time period. Newborn puppies need about 14 hours of sleep in the same period.

Puppy Facts...

Puppies require five small meals a day.

Puppy Facts...

Puppies' teeth begin to grow when they begin chewing, just like human babies.

Puppy Facts...

At one-year-old, a puppy is no longer considered a puppy -- it's considered an adult!

Puppy Facts...

A one-year-old puppy is the equivalent of a 15-year-old human.

Puppy Facts...

Touch is the first sense a puppy begins to use.

Puppy Facts...

The nose prints of a dog are as unique as a human's fingerprints.

Puppy Facts...

Many puppies mistake a human smile for aggressive behavior if the person shows his or her teeth when smiling.

Puppy Facts...

Once their sense glands develop, puppies can smell up to 1,000 times better than a human.

Puppy Facts...

Puppies don't open their eyes until they are nine to 12 days old.

Puppy Facts...

If your puppy bites or nips in play, you can often effectively train them out of this by saying 'ouch!' in a loud voice. This is a similar response to the yelps their littermates make when the same thing happens to them.

Puppy Facts...

Puppies may potentially be rejected by their mother if they are born by caesarean section and cleaned before being given back to them, as the dam may be unable to recognise the puppy as their own.

Puppy Facts...

When frightened or to indicate submission, dogs will tuck their tails between their legs- this is in order to cut off access to the scent glands around the anus, which carry identifying information about the dog which can easily be 'decoded' by other canines.

Puppy Facts...

The average dog is thought to be about as intelligent as the average two year old child, according to research by leading animal psychologists in America.

Puppy Facts...

Puppies only listen to the initial syllable of a word- So if your pup is named 'Princess Pretty Paws' then the only part of the name that your pup will come to recognise is 'Prin!'

Made in the USA
San Bernardino, CA
10 December 2017